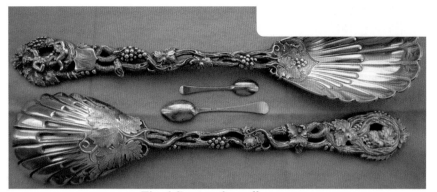

Fig. 1 *Serving & snuff spoons*

Collecting Silver

Breaks, Fakes & Assay Marks

Richard W Turner

Fig. 2 *Three salt & one snuff spoon.*

Fig. 3 *Enamelled spoons + cast spoon*

Contents

© Copyright 2011 Richard W Turner

Fig. 4 *A selection of 18ᵗʰ/early 19ᵗʰ Century spoons with later decoration.*
Front cover*: a group of interesting spoons, all with points of which to be aware.*

Introduction

Collecting and selling silver requires alertness on many fronts. Most are obvious – to someone with experience of silver built up over several years. Unfortunately, this is at its greatest importance, and least availability, during the initial creation of your collection, or establishment of your reputation as a dealer.

Some experiences on ebay, made me realise that there was an urgent need for a handy book on avoiding frauds and fakes, wear and breaks. Clarifying assay marks rapidly became another obvious necessity. My previous book on silver opened doors for accessing items held by some top dealers and collectors, which I have used for my illustrations. For this, I wish to extend my grateful thanks.

I would especially like to give my thanks for the help given to me by the London Assay Office, especially Dave Merry. The Birmingham, Sheffield and Edinburgh Assay Offices, the dealers at the London Silver Vaults and staff at the Bonhams, Boningtons, Lyon & Turnbull, Thomson Roddick & Medcalf, and Woolley & Wallis auction houses. I also wish to thank Nina Ball (who instigated and then proof read it), Wynyard Wilkinson, Miles Harrison, Trevor Downes, Mark Hamilton, William Walter, Ken Read, Colin Fraser, Peter Boughton, Nick Shaw, Mark and Gareth Turner and Ralph Pollard for their invaluable assistance.

Most silver available is in reasonable, or better, condition. The few points I have listed for your attention, will, I hope permit you to create the collection of your dreams, with minimal nightmares. Most importantly, enjoy collecting.

Richard W Turner. May 2011

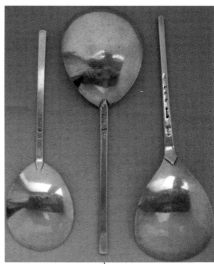

Figs. 5 & 6 *Slip top spoons, front and rear. Left: 20th Century reproduction; centre: actual 17th Century spoon; right: fake spoon, mid 18th century stem.*

3

Collecting Silver

Silver is such a wide subject that an excellent collection can be formed with a minimal or a massive outlay. In either case, to create a fully satisfying collection, a good understanding of the subject is desirable.

The cost of flatware (spoons, forks, etc.) can range from pennies up to thousands of pounds depending on your subject and pocket. Spoons vary in size from snuff to basting, from five to thirty-five centimetres long, with a wide range of patterns and decorations (*Fig. 1*). Hollow-ware (salts, tankards, teapots, etc.) requires a similar budget, but usually from a higher starting point. Occasionally, with a little luck, acceptable pieces of either can be found at a boot fair, for mere pennies.

The trigger for this book came from a pair of salt spoons bought on ebay, one having been repaired at some time in its history. This gave me the idea of alerting against some of the pitfalls in buying and selling and to recognise the best.

Fig. 7 *Good cast table spoons from 1760 & 1816 (top)*

Gain a good insight into the subject

Before beginning to collect antiques, ideally one should learn as much as possible about the subject. Read several books on silver, buying a few to assist and advise you in forming your collection.

Years ago, I read an article on silver that recommended assembling a selection of catalogues from auctions. The best are those with the majority of lots illustrated, with an attached description. Create a scrapbook, giving a double page of examples from each decade. Studying these can create an understanding of the way that fashions in silver have changed over the centuries, especially from the Eighteenth Century onwards. Get to know the changes and the prices.

This method of study also holds good for the building of any collection. The more you know, the better, with the added possibility that your knowledge could lead to employment, should you so wish. It also ensures that you are less likely to end up with too many examples for which you may be sorry later. As an extra advantage this deep knowledge can assist in spotting the odd "sleeper", which, when resold, can help to subsidise your collection.

If you are near London, visits to the London Silver Vaults, off Chancery Lane or a trip to Portobello Road on a Saturday morning, are very worthwhile. Take a walk round, just studying. In both places there is an extraordinarily wide range of silver-ware and expertise available. The theme of your future collection should soon come to you.

Buy the best quality that you can find and afford

Always buy the best quality pieces that you can find. If, or when, you change your topic, or require funds, your collection will then be of benefit, becoming the financial basis for your new collection. Remember, poor quality pieces are usually difficult to resell.

***Fig. 8** Iona style spoon & later copy (top).*   ***Fig. 9** Backs of spoons*

Figs. 8 & 9 display how standards have lowered over the years. The original hand-wrought Iona-style jam spoon (bottom) was made in 1896; the attempt to cast a copy was made some sixty years later.

As the handle of the copy is thinner and weaker, it had to be soldered at the neck. The pattern on the front of the handle has come out poorly, and the decorative hammer marks on the back of the bowl have been virtually lost.

***Figs. 10 & 11** Top, King's Pattern, single struck, with a poor replacement bowl compared with another of similar age. Note the shape and difference in patina.*

At times, due to rarity, a poor quality piece may be the only one available to fill a hole in your collection. *Fig. 10* shows one such example. The repaired spoon is a scarce Scottish Provincial example. Its cost was only a fraction of that for a good one, thus, it should be profitably resalable, when one finds the perfect example. "Single struck" indicates that it only has the pattern struck on one side.

Initially, while forming the nucleus of your collection, the urge to buy is incredibly strong. Too often, new collectors are tempted to purchase two or three lesser items, rather than one good one. Later, as the collection progresses, it will be difficult to recover this outlay, or to regain the missed prime example.

Everybody makes mistakes. If you can learn from them, there is always the saving grace that it was money well spent, after all.

Never be over-eager, or impatient

If you let drop how keen you are to buy an item for some reason, if no price-tag is attached, it is not unknown for a slight "inflation" to occur.

Shop around and do not buy the first example that you see, unless it is in first class condition, and the right price.

Never under-value other people

Never believe that you know more than everybody else. You will always find someone whose speciality knowledge is just what you need. Often they will be only too happy to help – as long as you refrain from getting up their noses first!

Similarly, do not be too ready to over-value people. They may believe that they know a subject, but their information may be totally wrong. Their pricing may be high, but that does not mean that their valuation is correct, even if they have managed to sell similar pieces.

Damaged items can be ideal for use

Fig. 12 Uneven, scarred tines　　*Fig. 13 Tines poorly evened off (top)*

Be alert to wear on spoon bowls and fork tines. These are all too often discarded for scrap. With a little work, they can be rejuvenated. I enjoy my breakfast cereal off a slightly battered dessert spoon, my dinner with a table fork with realigned and re-shaped tines, and my dessert with a teaspoon which has been

6

slightly bent at some time. My enjoyment is from the fact that all were made by an early 19th Century London silversmith named Richard Turner, sadly no relation.

A little research can give a lot of extra satisfaction and fun in collecting.

Fig. 14 Good & worn bowls   *Fig. 15* Bent bowl

Crests and engraving

It used to be the fashion to erase crests and the initials of former owners from silver. Fortunately, fashion has now changed to retaining them, so that we can fully enjoy the history of a piece. With a little research, you may find, from the crest and date letter, that the item that you are holding may have originally been owned by one of the heroes of Waterloo.

Old crests are worth studying to observe the skill of the shading in the creation of the picture, as well as maybe discovering to whom they belonged and if there are any anomalies.

Fig. 16   *Fig. 17*   *Fig. 18*   *Fig. 19*

Fig. 16 a lion rampant; used by a wide range of possible families.
Fig. 17 displays the crest of a spur with wings attached, and the motto "Never Unprepared", with the Scottish Saltire, indicating a Johnston family (20th Century).
Fig. 18 has a squirrel holding a water-bouget, which was the crest of the Nicholls family of Mershland, Norfolk.
Fig. 19 is a bull's head, cabossed (no part of the neck shown), possibly Bradley.

| **Fig. 20** | **Fig. 21** | **Fig. 22** | **Fig. 23** |

Fig. 20 is possibly a pun, displaying a deer with a heart – a branch of the Hart family?

Fig. 21 is a typical late 17th Century wedding engraving.

Fig. 22 has a bull's head out of the coronet of a marquess. Interestingly, this should be a ducal coronet; possibly from a service belonging to a duke's eldest son.

Fig. 23 displays a lion below an earl's coronet. This lion is often for the Howard family, but that, again, should have a ducal coronet, so further research would be required. (Information resourced from Fairbairn's *Book of Crests*.)

Cleaning

Some old silver, when offered for sale, is in a highly polished condition. Sometimes, this is in response to the demands of buyers. Often, however, this polishing is to disguise the fact that the item has been "attended to". Dents or engravings may have been removed, the tines or bowl were worn and have been re-shaped, or there may even have been a solder repair. Always examine these pieces with great care.

Silver is like wood, slowly gaining a patina with age, assuming a deeper, darker colouration. Hand polished, it will gleam and you will see its life. The polisher, however, tends to have grubby hands. If a buffing machine or some of the modern, long lasting cleaners are used, the job is done rapidly and less messily. Sadly, the only proof then remaining of its age will be the assay mark. With the loss of the patination, built up over the centuries, all the history is gone. Do you want to be flash or to retain the history?

Cracks, wear & solder repairs

Solder repairs are usually simple to spot. A useful way to reveal the existence of any repairs is to run the fingers along the sides of a piece. Even with a good repair, you can usually feel a slight swelling. This can be felt as a slight change in the metal, like a bruise on a leg. Another excellent way to detect a join is to breath hard on the area. Condensation will reveal any area where the silver is of a different constitution. In larger pieces, there will be a detectable difference in the surface (*Figs. 41 & 42*).

Are the tines of a fork worn down, uneven or damaged? Is there uneven wear on the bowl? Are all the joints on a toast-rack firm and smooth? Are the legs misshapen? Are there holes worn in the silver sheet?

Fig. 24 *Hanoverian spoon, stem cracked*

Fig. 25 *Lengthways split*

Cracks are often found on the stem of older spoons and forks, where they were hallmarked. The impact of the punch hitting it would have weakened the silver there (*Fig. 24*). A high risk potential weak point on spoons is at the join between the bowl and stem, where maximum pressure is exerted (*Fig. 26*).

Check on teaspoons at the widest part of the bowl. Excess pressure, at some time on thinner spoons, can cause a bend at that point (see *Fig. 15*.)

Is the bowl of the spoon worn at the tip, dented, or is the stem bent? Are there solder marks (*Fig. 27*), or is it merely wear from condiment bottles (*Fig. 28*)?

Fig. 26 *Neck repair*   **Fig. 27** *Stem repair*   **Fig. 28** *Condiment spoon wear*

On some pieces, the maker's mark may be indistinct; often this is due to wear or repair. In other cases it could be due to the punch being poorly struck or even worn. Study carefully and make your decision.

Collect items that you like

Most importantly, if you buy items that you like, they will give you pleasure and value for money, irrespective of any vagaries in fashion.

The values of some items do go up and down with popular taste. If you buy solely for investment, a year later, it may be worth only half the price paid.

Registered Design Numbers

The Registration Diamond Mark was first introduced in Britain in 1842. Its aim was to ensure that designs could not be copied without the permission of the owner. It also allowed the public to be certain that the goods they were buying were actually British. The first diamond marks covered the period 1842 to 1867, and the second from 1868 to 1883. These were then superceded by the Registered Design Numbers, which continued until 1965. Further information can be found on-line.

From these marks, the date of registration of the design, and by whom, can be ascertained. *Fig. 29* shows an example of the second series. "I" indicates metal, 27 January 1870, parcel number 9. In *Fig. 30*, the design was registered in 1899, and this item was made by Levi & Saloman of Birmingham and assayed in 1901.

Fig. 29 *Registered Diamond Mark*   **Fig. 30** *Registered Design Number*

Terminology

Ian Pickford's book *"Silver Flatware 1660-1980"*, gives a comprehensive coverage of the terminology relating to various sections of silver flatware.

Fig. 31 shows a small range of condiment, mustard and salt spoons (top left round to bottom right). The handles on condiment spoons were elongated to reach inside cruet bottles, having various shapes to the bowls. Mustard spoons had elongated bowls while salt spoons had a deep round or oval bowl, often gilt flashed. This gilt was to protect the silver from corrosion from the salt.

Recently, there has been a new trend with salt spoons over 8cms long being termed "Master Salt Spoons". This is probably to encourage the sale of single antique spoons, trying to hide the fact that they were originally part of a set of four or six.

Antique condiment spoons were much larger than those used today. This was because substantial quantities of spices were required to conceal the fact that, due to the lack of refrigeration, food was sometimes not quite as fresh as one could desire.

Fig. 31 *From top left, anti-clockwise: fiddle & thread pattern condiment ladle, American c1830; ornate condiment spoon, Birmingham 1911; Old English pattern condiment spoon, London 1810; fiddle pattern mustard spoon, London 1852; Old English machine bright-cut mustard spoon, Birmingham 1885; trefid repro mustard spoon, Birmingham 1878; Onslow salt spoon, Birmingham 1899; Grecian pattern salt spoon, London 1870; pointed end salt spoon, Banff c1790; King's Husk salt spoon, London 1822.*

Changes in spoon design

Fig. 32 *Trefid*   *Fig. 33* *Dognose*

Most Trefid spoons were made in the late Seventeenth Century. In the first decade of the Eighteenth Century, this evolved into the Dognose shape, so called due to the form of the end of the terminal. Both these types had a tapering strap on the back of the bowl, like a rat-tail, hence the common term. The rat-tail was sometimes decorated on later spoons.

Fig. 34 *Hanoverian*   *Fig. 35* *Old English*

11

The Hanoverian shape appeared around 1710, lasting into the third quarter of the century. The rat-tail was replaced by assorted drops, and then picture backs. The end of the handle was turned up, being laid bowl down on the table. The Old English shape appeared about 1760, having the end of the handle curved down. These were laid with the bowl up, hence the respective positions of the engravings.

***Fig. 36** Fiddle*   ***Fig. 37** King's Shape*

The vast majority of British Fiddle Pattern was made after 1800, with King's Shape appearing in about 1815. Many other patterns evolved from these.

Auctions

Auctions are an excellent source for collectors, usually, with convenient viewing times. In most auctions, if you wish to bid, you must register, receiving a bidding number. This is to validate those bidding and ensure correct allocation of lots.

Check on the estimates. It is worth visiting an auction to ensure that those given are fairly accurate. When you find any lots of interest to you, decide how much you wish to pay for them. You can leave a bid, bid live or bid on-line.

Most Auction Houses have a "buyers' premium", varying between 15 - 25%. This has to be added to the price that you pay, and usually has VAT added. If the premium is 17%, you will pay a total of 21% on top of your bid, so, if your bid was for £50, you end up paying £60.50.

Often, one of the hardest parts of live bidding is ensuring that you do not get carried away and exceed the highest amount that you wish to bid. To restrain yourself, you can leave a bid with the auctioneer, or one of the staff. Should you leave your bid with a porter, it is normal for you to give them a tip.

Often, these days, there are several pieces in a lot, of which you may only desire one. Ebay, as well as being a convenient source for collectable pieces, is an excellent way of disposing of the remnants. With silver, the assay mark is often of great interest. To display this, the majority of modern digital cameras have a macro mode, indicated by a tulip-shaped indicator, plus anti-shake mode. If these are selected, good close-up photographs of these marks are readily attainable.

Examine purchases carefully

Know exactly what you are buying, always examine items very carefully. Look for cracks, dents, repairs. Has an engraving been removed? Is it as it was made or have there been later changes? Has wear been disguised?

Wear & Repairs

Tines on antique forks are often unevenly worn; with scars due to sharp steel knives cutting in as tough pieces of meat were attacked (*Figs. 12 & 13*). The tine area should be just over twice as long as it is wide, tapering, symmetrically, to points. Worn ones can still be unobtrusively rectified for use today. This recycling allows you to gain excellent pieces of tableware, whilst, as a plus if crested, creating interesting conversation pieces. Well-balanced, brand new plated flatware is almost as expensive. A downside is that silverware must not be placed in the dishwasher, however, the satisfaction of eating off silver more than compensates.

It is not uncommon for antique silver spoons to have unattractive wear on the left end of the bowl (*Fig. 14*). It is predominantly on this side because everyone was right handed, or forced to be so, thus scraping that edge of the bowl on the plate. Other detractions are dents in the bowl, caused by having something dropped on them, or little nicks on the edges. It is relatively easy for this minor damage to be smoothed off or removed, restoring the aesthetic balance of the object.

Fig. 38 Caddy spoon damage

Fig. 39 Salt shovel damage

Fig. 40 Hanoverian spoons. Top: bowl barely worn. Centre: bowl worn down, narrowed and thinned. Bottom: bowl re-shaped to hide the amount of wear. Originally the bowls would have been of similar size and shape.

With older collectable spoons, caution must be taken with any repairs. Bad wear reduces the value, so, in some cases the size of bowl has been reduced to improve the appearance. Usually, the spoon is then polished to hide all evidence of the work, also removing the patination of centuries. This re-shaping of the bowl reduces the size. In an Eighteenth Century Hanoverian table spoon, the size of the bowl should be approximately 7.7cm long by 4.2cm wide. In the case of the three spoons in *Fig. 40*, the top spoon is almost unworn. The centre, worn down drastically over the years, has the bowl now 7.1 by 3.9cm. The bottom spoon has had the bowl reshaped to remove uneven signs of wear, now 6.8 by 4.1cm.

Salt spoons with a shell bowl (*see Fig. 39*) also have weaknesses. The bowl was made of thin gauge metal so that it could be easily pressed into shape. This one, made circa 1770, has come under strain, or been stepped on, at some time, with the result that there is a solder repair and cracks along some of the struts.

All five collectable spoons pictured on the front cover have faults. The top and bottom ones were decorated later, coming under the term "berry spoons", to be dealt with in the next chapter. The cast fruit server has a repair and a small crack (*Figs. 41 to 44*). The bowl of the rat-tail has been reshaped to remove signs of wear (*Fig. 40* bottom), and the caddy spoon is damaged (*Fig. 38*). Always examine carefully before purchasing or bidding.

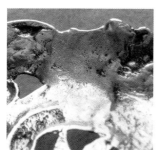 

Figs. 41 & 42 *Fruit spoon, back and top sides, showing excess solder giving a different surface at the back and excess blob of solder at the front.*

Figs. 43 & 44 *Crack near the handle, viewed from both sides.*

Cracks across the stems of old forks and spoons are sometimes found (*see Fig. 24*). Often, as in this case, the crack was caused by the assay punch creating a weakness, which then deteriorates over the years. It is possible to clean and then solder the crack, but, in this case, it would be unwise as it would detract more from the picture back spoon. Occasionally, due to the impact of the assay punches, over time, cracks develop down the stem (*Fig. 25*). This reduces the value in both cases.

Other cracks can occur in the stems, if they come under stress from bending (*see Figs. 45-47*). Cracks on the bowls, especially where the handle joins can be soldered, but will be noticeable and diminish the value – except as a useable spoon. A further weakness on spoons is if the bowl is bent from being trapped or used as a lever (*Fig. 15*). With great care this could be straightened and the kinks hammered out, but this usually still leaves a weakness.

Fig 45 Fractured teaspoon.

Fig 46 Stress fracture, top view

Fig. 47 Stress fracture, right side of stem.

Fig. 48 Butter knife blade separation

Dessert knives and forks with filled handles must be inspected very carefully to ensure that the blades are not loose or partially detached from the handles (*Fig. 48*). The handles must also be checked for dents or wear as these cannot be rectified.

The weakest point of sugar tongs is at the bow. Check to ensure that they are not bent or repaired. If they are bent there, the bowls may not meet up properly.

Fig. 49 Repaired sifter inside bowl

Fig. 50 External view of repair

Ladles and sifters, when made, were elegant and balanced. *Fig. 49* shows one that has obviously been repaired. The handle should be more than twice as long as it is now. On the inside of the bowl, traces of solder can be seen where the piercing was resoldered. On the outside, blobs of solder can be seen to the right of the drop and where the remnant of the beaded-edge handle was joined back (*Fig. 50*). This item was made in about 1770, when it was bottom marked which may have helped to trigger some of the damage. The result of this poor repair is that there is now no assay mark, and we have been left with an ungainly piece.

Filled and ivory handles

Check the handles of shoe horns, button hooks, knives and other silver handled tools for wear. In the case of knives and forks, check the handles for fitting. *Fig. 48* is a butter knife, which has probably been placed in a dishwasher or very hot water. The handle filling has softened, and the blade has moved.

Fig. 51 *Fork, dented handle*   **Fig. 52** *Ivory knife handle crack*

A further problem arises when the handle has been dented, as any dents or holes cannot be rectified.

Ivory handles should be checked for splits along the ivory (*Fig. 52*), again often caused by hot water. The split is discoloured with age for part of its length, but the last part is almost unnoticeable. Also check that the ferrule, the silver sheet covering the join between ivory and blade, is undamaged and does not rotate.

Salts

Sodium chloride (common table salt) reacts with silver, corroding it. Old salt spoons had gilt bowls to stop this, as corrosion on salts and salt spoons leaves them blackened, similar to rust on iron. This can be removed, but often with difficulty, and great care must be taken not to wear through the silver.

Fig. 53 *Salt corroded*   **Fig. 54** *Pepperette damage to base and neck*

16

Always inspect salts very carefully. Ensure that corrosion has not eaten into the metal, leaving holes or thinning. (See *Fig. 53,* pieces of paper have been inserted through corrosion holes, right rim.) Look for dents or other signs of damage on the base, with legs bent from an impact or dropping. Examine for solder or stretch marks around each leg. There may be a tell-tale bulge inside the bowl.

Mirrors, photo frames and lids

In *Fig. 55,* the dressing table bottle top on the left is perfect, while the one on the right has been crushed at some time.

Toast rack struts (*Fig. 56*) should be checked for cracks, breaks and repairs.

Fig. 55 *Damaged bottle top*   ***Fig. 56*** *Toast rack strut*   ***Fig. 57*** *Pot lid damage*

Silver backed mirrors, photo frames and lids for dressing table bottles are often heavily embossed. As they were high profile and kept in view for enjoyment and use, they were regularly polished. Those of the Twentieth Century were often made of thin silver sheet, which rapidly wore down with cleaning. This resulted in little holes occurring, none of which can be repaired. Due to the ornamentation, this is often difficult to notice initially, especially if it has not been polished.

Fig. 57 shows the lid from a hair pin jar, which looks attractive when on the jar, whilst the rim is slightly crushed, with holes in the top. *Figs. 58 & 59* show the silver from a mirror of 1910, held against a solid surface, as if still whole, and then against the light to show the wear.

Fig. 58 *Mirror-back against surface*   ***Fig. 59*** *Silver held against the light*

17

Frauds, Fakes and Forgeries

Most spurious examples encountered in collecting silver arise from frauds, rather than fakes or forgeries. At the lower end of the market, (under £100) a faked or forged piece is not economically viable. Most can be spotted with minimal experience. If something is much cheaper than you expect, be very suspicious. Usually there will be an excellent reason – faked, repaired or stolen.

Faking silver items carries a very stiff prison sentence, and it is illegal to even own a faked piece of silver. Should you ever suspect that a piece in your possession is fake contact the nearest Assay Office as soon as possible.

In some respects, much Victorian plated ware could be said to be fraud, but legal. Most made before 1896 had marks carefully created to resemble silver marks (*Figs. 60-65*). Some makers applied the crown to plated wares, so buyers could keep up with the "Joneses", but at a reasonable price. Another ploy with Birmingham-made nickel plated flatware was to create grandiloquent names, like "Nevada", "Bengal", "Argentine" and "Brazilian Silver" from Daniel & Arter and "Potosi Silver" from the Potosi Silver Co (Levi & Salaman).

This was ceased in 1896 by an Act of Parliament, probably forced through by those who could afford silver, and it is eminently possible that some of the "Joneses" would have been among the MPs passing the Act.

Fig. 60 Brazilian Silver nickel plate   *Fig. 61* Nevada silver nickel plate

Fig. 62 Potosi silver   *Fig. 63* Daniel & Arter plated

Fig. 64 J Gilbert electro plated   *Fig. 65* pre-1896 plated mark

Fig. 66 800 plated jam spoon   *Fig. 67* German silver assay mark

Continental manufacturers were just as guilty. Just because it has 800 stamped on it does not necessarily indicate that it is 80% silver. Some plated items have an incuse marking of 800 stamped on them. This is similar to German marks except that real German silver also has the moon and crown mark (*Figs. 66 & 67*).

Learn to tell the difference between the feel of silver and that of plated wares. Silver is springy, with give to it, plated wares feel hard.

Other fakes were Colonial and China Trade silver, which were sometimes lower grade silver. These were often punched to emulate English marks as closely as possible (*Figs. 68 & 69*).

Fig. 68 *Canadian mark c1850*

Fig. 69 *China Trade mark*

Always be aware of designation errors in auction catalogues. Table spoons were used as soup spoons prior to the First World War. Nowadays, they are commonly used as serving spoons, and are often termed as such. As a rough guide, table spoons are approximately 20cm long, while a real serving spoon measures 23-35cm long, dessert spoons are around 18cm, teaspoons less than 15cm and coffee spoons less than 10cm.

The so-called "berry spoons" are also frauds rather than fakes. These were usually plain Old English, or even Hanoverian pattern spoons, which were cleaned before being placed in a press, which embossed a pretty pattern on the bowl, sometimes also leaving bright cut marks on the front of the stem (*see Fig. 70*).

Fig. 70 *Top, 18th Century bright cut teaspoon. Centre, 18th Century spoon with later decoration. Bottom, 20th Century, machine decorated spoon.*

In Victorian times, entrepreneurs were making fabulous profits from the Colonies to a level only dreamt of by today's bankers. To their annoyance, while possessing these fortunes, they were dismissed as "nouveau riche" or "Trade."

Snobbishness was rife. Mere funds were nothing compared to a title. A few of the richer English and American merchants sold their daughters, with a massive dowry, to an easily found impoverished Lord, to get the cachet. Others, thinking a little better of their daughters, or failing to sell, still longed for Respect.

The easy way was to create your own family history. Take a set of old flatware, tart it up and claim that it has been in the family for generations. Sadly, late Seventeenth and Eighteenth Century examples were plain, while flamboyance was the mode in the last quarter of the Nineteenth Century (*Fig. 1* serving spoons).

Laid out on the dining table, spoons were an obvious target. To decorate them as berry spoons required a simple press. Gilding was applied to give that even richer finish. The true reason for the gilding was to hide the fact that they had been heated and annealed so they were sufficiently malleable for the stamping. If they were not annealed, they would have become stressed and very brittle.

Fig. 70 shows the differences between original hand engraved bright cut, much later machine engraving and the impressed effort. The latter's variation in the accuracy of positioning of the pattern and marks at the back are often apparent.

A selection of the range of later decorations applied to spoons is shown in *Fig. 4*. The berry patterns are the easiest and cheapest, and are still being carried out today, no longer for fashion, merely to multiply the price. Those wishing to really impress would have had them hand or machine engraved or a special die could have been cut to impress the decoration.

As well as berry spoons, there are some that were decorated later with engraved patterns, but these are scarcer as it was a much more expensive process. While some spoons were hand decorated, at this time machine engraving appeared (*Fig. 72*). As can be seen, the balanced hand-cutting of *Fig. 71* is far superior.

Fig. 71 *18ᵗʰ Century bright-cut table spoon*

Fig. 72 *20ᵗʰ Century machine decorated table spoon.*

A full hand-decorated canteen would have cost an enormous sum – more than a hundred pounds (twice as much as a country vicar's stipend, or a small cottage). Social manoeuvring was paramount; so this cost was of minimal importance to them. When you have thousands coming in, appearance is of prime consequence, in order to keep it coming, not unknown in today's bonus-driven culture.

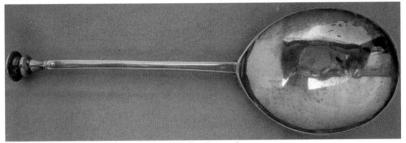

Fig. 73 Seal top front.

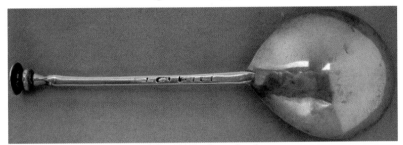

Fig. 74 Seal top back

Over the last thirty years, Seventeenth Century spoons have become targets for the fakers. Twenty years ago, there were many poor fakes on the market, see the slip top and seal top spoons in *Figs. 5 & 73.*

Most of these fakes are easily recognised. The criminals had a poor grasp of their subject, but were able to find victims at the same level. They utilised stems from early Eighteenth Century pieces. However, slip tops were only made over the period from 1625 to 1640, so one with a 1740 assay mark should immediately ring alarm bells.

In *Figs. 5 & 6*, we have an original Daniel Carey slip top from 1630; an illegal fake piece made with a Marmaduke Daintrey stem, c1750, and a Thomas Bradbury Twentieth Century reproduction. Sitting side by side, you can see the difference in the patination.

The stem of the forgery is too thin. The bowl shows hammer marks and is also not thick enough. It was probably hammered out from a typical dessert spoon, with the drop filed down to the diamond shape. Finally, the colouring is very harsh,

21

compared with the deep sheen of the untouched Eighteenth Century section, after almost 300 years of use, cleaning and general reaction with the atmosphere.

The Twentieth Century reproduction is nicely polished, but there is no depth to the polish, leaving it a much lighter colour.

An even more blatant effort is the seal top (*Fig. 73*). This has the stem from a mid-eighteenth century fork, with the maker's mark and date letter deliberately rubbed. It is too thin, the solder mark is obvious by the seal top, and there are file marks on the stem by the hallmarks. Though the bowl is roughly the correct size at 5.5 by 6.5cms, it is far too thin, and the patination is completely wrong.

Fig. 75 *Fake apostle front*

Fig. 76 *Apostle back.*

The apostle spoon (*Fig. 75*) is a better job, but still comparatively easy to spot. The stem is clearly marked for London 1740, which is a century too late. The solder fire stain where the apostle was added is difficult to detect, but shows it to be the wrong style of connection. Further warning signs are that the bowl is much too thin and shows clear signs of hammer work. Finally, the patination of the bowl does not match that of the stem. In all these cases, the items should have their marks obliterated, or be re-assayed, to be legally owned.

Many reproduction apostle spoons were imported from the Continent and are perfectly legal, as are British examples, when correctly assayed.

Stilton scoops are often created by taking a table or dessert spoon and bending up the sides. These are then sawn to give an undulating pattern. A real stilton scoop should be of heavier gauge to scoop out the cheese without bending.

Fig. 77 is an example of a converted dessert spoon. The trimming of the silver is quite rough and uneven, with file marks on the edges, and the bowl is too thin to be practical. There are also some scratches on the bowl from where it was held to be bent inwards while re-shaping.

Fig. 77 *Stilton scoop converted from a dessert spoon*

Fig. 78 *Front of "snuff spoon"*

Fig. 79 *Back of "snuff spoon"*

Figs. 78 & 79 show the front and back of an example which was called a "snuff spoon", though it was more likely converted for drugs. The remnant of the assay mark is on the same side as the bowl and the "back" is decorated. This indicates that it was originally one leg from a pair of sugar nips. Examples like those shown in *Figs. 77 & 78* should be re-assayed due to change of use.

I once saw, at the V&A, a small helmet cream jug, allegedly made by Hester Bateman, which was a forgery. The real assay mark had been removed, and then replaced with her mark off a teaspoon, which had been soldered into place. It was adequately done, but relatively easy to spot, with experience.

The Assay Office in London runs a very interesting seminar on fakes and forgeries occasionally. You get a whole day, including lunch, being taught many ways to spot expert fakes, at the same time actually getting to hold them and inspect them at close quarters. Having been on one, I can personally recommend this as a very enjoyable and worthwhile day.

23

British silver marks and their history

Fig. 80 *London hollow-ware mark*   **Fig. 81** *London flatware mark*

Modern London assay marks consist of four punch marks. The first has two, or more, letters, for the maker or sponsor's mark, usually their initials. The next mark is the sterling silver mark, a lion standing on three legs with the right front paw raised. The third mark is the London town mark, a leopard's head. The final mark is a single letter to indicate the date of assay. *Fig. 80* shows an example of a 1918 box made by Sampson Morden & Co. *Fig. 81* is a 1902 spoon by West & Son, showing the differences in punch orientation for hollow-ware and flatware.

English silver has been assayed to confirm its purity since the reign of Edward I. Date letters, first introduced in London in 1478 during the reign of Edward IV, identify the date of manufacture of each piece of silver. These assist various themes for collecting, e.g. family or national anniversaries.

Prior to 1700, many towns in England had working silversmiths. Several even had a town guild and mark, but most were unofficial, and thus not authorised to touch (test) the standard of the metal. By 1730, the majority of these towns were sending their wares to be tested at the nearest major Assay Office.

Scotland, however, was a different matter. There were a number of towns, having specific town marks, where smiths formed guilds and trained apprentices. Of these, very few ever sent any of their silver for assay. Despite new laws, this continued in some towns, even after 1830. Initially, the reasons for not sending items away for assay had been to safeguard against goods being damaged en route, or, worse, stolen, by one of the marauding bands still rampant after the Jacobite risings.

From 1784, when duty had to be paid on every ounce worked, lack of assay made a large saving. In Scotland, this duty was even more unpopular, as it went to the English Government, the 1715 and 1745 rebellions being still fresh in many Scottish minds.

Ireland had its main assay office in Dublin, but there were also thriving guilds of smiths in Cork and Limerick.

Fig. 82 *London Britannia marks for 1714, maker Isaac Dalton*

At the end of the Seventeenth Century, after the Civil War, silver coinage was still in short supply. Some silversmiths made this worse by using it as a cheap source of silver, clipping the edges of coins or even melting them down to create plate. To prevent this, in 1697 the Government raised the silver standard for plate to 97.25% (Britannia standard). In 1700, because many smiths were still ignoring this Law, a further Act was brought in affecting all the Assay Offices. Several closed, and the majority of silver items we see today are from this period onwards.

After 1700, seven official Assay Offices remained working in Britain; London, Chester, Dublin, Edinburgh, Exeter, Newcastle and York. York closed in 1713, reopening in 1778. Silversmiths were working in Glasgow, but it was not an Assay Office until 1819. Of the present Assay Offices, Birmingham and Sheffield were not opened until 1773.

Some pieces of Georgian and Victorian silver bear a further small punched mark. These were added by the journeyman smiths, while working for a sponsor, to denote that it was their work, and not that of the sponsor, whose initials the item bore. These marks can be found on silver from all of the towns.

Fig. 83 1791   *Fig. 84* 1847   *Fig. 85* 1863   *Fig. 86* 1885
Examples of four 18th & 19th Century journeyman marks

The majority of these punch-marks were small, neat and unobtrusive, but the mark in *Fig. 87* is an anomaly. This star-shaped mark, on a Lias & Son teaspoon, was the same size as the duty mark, much larger than usual. Whoever struck it was either incompetent or in a very bad mood, as the punch was hit hard enough to leave a dent that can be seen in the metal on the front of the spoon.

 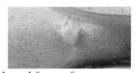

Figs. 87 & 88 Photo of star punch back and front of spoon

If it was done by a journeyman and he had just been sacked, he definitely left his mark. Another alternative is that it may have been struck for an owner previously robbed by guests or staff. This mark would have been to ensure that nobody else stole any of his property. Sadly, I saw only the single spoon, but, if it was done to the whole set, it would be more likely to corroborate the latter idea. I find that little things like this help to give added enjoyment to collecting.

In a few cases, the date or town of manufacture can be difficult to identify. Some assay marks vary merely in the shape of the shield on one or more of the elements. It is always worth carrying one of the small books, listing these marks, to identify the origins.

Some upper and lower case letters are very similar (o, s, v and w); also the Gothic letters C, D, E, G, O, and Q. In some cases, the duty mark can help solve the problem. An open mind must be retained, as to which letter it is, before carefully checking in your book of assay marks.

***Fig. 89** Possibly confusing Gothic letters C, D, E, G, O, Q*

Town Marks

London

When Edward I instituted standards for gold and silver in 1300, the fact was denoted by items being struck with what is termed "the uncrowned leopard's head". This mark is actually a lion's head. This confusion arose from the heraldic term "leopart" being short for "lion passant guardant". This mark was initially to be struck on all items assayed "throughout the realm". Later it became solely the London town mark. In 1478, a crown was added to the leopard's head when the gold standard dropped from 19.2 to 18 carats.

***Fig. 90** 1762 silver marks, crowned leopard's head*

From 1784 until 1890, there were up to five separate marks on London silver. Prior to 1820, on smaller spoons, the leopard's head was often omitted, due to space constraints (*Fig. 93*).

Before 1781, each mark was separately punched, low on the stem, near the bowl (bottom marking). After that date, the Assay Offices began to use a fly press, a combination punch holding the three or four town punches, giving precise alignment. At this time the position of punching moved up towards the end of the handle (top marking). The sponsors or makers then added their own mark. Prior to 1780, on smaller spoons, the maker's mark and the lion passant were usually the only marks punched, to prove that it was of the correct silver content. This was due to lack of space, and to prevent damage from the punches.

The full set of marks on London pieces of silver, holding the bowl in the left hand, reading from the right (right-handed punching), consisted of:

1. The maker's, or sponsor's, mark. This consisted of two or more letters denoting the initials of the name or names. A famous example of a sponsor was Hester Bateman, whose mark was HB in script. She never worked on the silver herself, employing a number of journeymen to do that. Prior to 1720, most silver was marked with the first two letters of the surname. Some items have the original maker's mark over-struck by another smith, denoting that the later smith was the seller. This stock may have been acquired due to bankruptcy, death, or merely to fill an order.

2. The mark generally referred to as the leopard's head. This was crowned from 1478 until 1821, and uncrowned since 1821. Over the years, there have been many changes in the leopard's head, especially in the early 18th Century.

***Fig. 91** 1821 crowned leopard*

***Fig. 92** 1821 uncrowned leopard*

3. The lion passant guardant, from 1550 until 1697, and 1 June 1720 until May 1821, and the lion passant from 1821 until the present, denoting that the piece is of 92.5% silver. A lion passant guardant is a lion walking right to left (*Fig. 91*), but looking to the side – on guard. The lion passant is walking right to left, but looking ahead (*Fig. 92*). This mark was first introduced in 1544.

4. The date letter. This was an alphabetical mark, updated each year in May. In 1975, the changeover date became January 1st. Should you wish to obtain a piece of silver commemorating the accession to the throne of Queen Elizabeth II, it would be Q, for 1951/2 (February 6th). To celebrate her coronation, it would be S (June 2nd 1953). The date letter changed on 19 May, because that was St Dunstan's Day, the patron saint of goldsmiths.[1]

5. Other marks found on pieces are:

a) The Duty mark. This was the head of the monarch, stamped on silver to show that duty had been paid. This mark ceased to be applied in 1890, when duty was abolished.

b) There were later optional marks celebrating the Jubilee of King George V and Queen Mary and the Coronation and Jubilee of Queen Elizabeth II.

[1] St. Dunstan, was an excellent choice as patron saint of goldsmiths. Though the son of a Tenth Century Saxon nobleman, during his youth, he was a blacksmith, also working in gold and silver. He later became a monk, and, eventually, Archbishop of Canterbury.

c) From 1867 until 1904, "F" was punched on imported silver (*Fig. 103*)

As well as the date letter and maker's mark, Britannia Standard pieces were stamped with Britannia and a lion's head erased. (Erased, in armorial terms, means torn off, with jagged ends.) In 1720, the Sterling standard returned, but occasionally pieces are still made at Britannia standard (*Fig. 94*).

Fig. 93 short marks London 1797   ***Fig. 94*** Britannia mark London 1921

Methods of identifying date by punches

The Britannia Standard was introduced on 27 March 1697. The order of marks used was date letter; lion's head erased; Britannia; maker's mark (*Fig. 82*).

On 28 May 1716, the lion's head erased and Britannia marks were transposed, to indicate the tightening up of the assaying after a number of sub-standard articles were found in 1715.

1 June 1720, the Sterling Standard returned where the lion's head erased was replaced by the leopard's head crowned, and the Britannia mark replaced by the lion passant guardant (*Fig. 95*). Several different crowned leopards' heads, all hairy, were used between 1720 and 1728, but the shield shape remained constant. In 1729, when a Duty of six pence an ounce was introduced, the town mark shield changed to being pointed at the base.

Fig. 95 Sterling standard 1722

In 1736, the leopard head altered, becoming less hairy (*Fig. 96*). In 1739, the leopard head changed again as did its shield shape, contoured to the shape of the crowned leopard. The lion passant guardant's shield also changed to follow the shape of the animal.

In 1756, the date letters changed to Gothic capitals A–U (*Fig. 89*). The leopard's head and its shield changed, as did the shield for the lion.

On the 1st December 1784, a duty of six pence an ounce was reintroduced. This was an imposition of about 10%, silver being worth about five shillings an ounce. Payment was denoted by a punch of the king's head. Initially, this was incuse (*Fig. 97*), which goes deeper into the item. As this weakened many pieces, they ceased using it on the 24th July 1785. For the rest of the year, there was no duty mark. It was decided that the following year, from the 29th May, they would use a cameo duty mark, which could be incorporated in a block with the others.

Fig. 96 *Assay marks for1736*

Fig. 97 *1785 Incuse marks*

Fig. 98 *1797 incised duty*   **Fig. 99** *1804*   **Fig. 100** *1815 3rd duty mark*

In 1797, to help pay for the war against France, the duty was doubled to one shilling an ounce on silver, coming into effect on 6 July. To denote that the duty had been paid, the duty punch had cusp-like incisions into the field of the mark at the side and base (*Fig. 98*), (pre-duty *Fig. 93*).

In 1804, a further rise in duty to one shilling and threepence (25%) was imposed on 10 October. This time, an incision was made in the base (*Fig. 99*). On 14 June 1817, Ireland, where only one shilling an ounce had been paid until then, had its duty standardised at one shilling and threepence and, again, an incision was made in the base of the duty punch. A further rise to one shilling and sixpence came on 31 August 1817, at which time, the base of the duty punch was flattened, removing the incision (*Fig. 100*).

Occasionally, items appear without a maker's mark, possibly due to the maker's lack of time or merely having mislaid his punch. Others are found with the maker's mark inverted, probably caused by an inability to read by the smith.

Some pieces were made by larger sponsors, assayed, and then sold on for others to sell to the public. These pieces could have the final dealer's mark added, sometimes by over-stamping the original mark.

Further changes were in 1834, when the duty bust changed to that of William IV, then in 1836, the leopard's head changed.

On 20 June 1837, Victoria came to the throne, however the duty mark was not changed until the following year, as the punches had already been bought. There were then also alterations in the leopard head and the lion passant (*Fig. 101*).

29

Fig. 101 *London 1838 (C)*

Fig. 102 *London 1840 (E)*

In 1840, William Wyon became the engraver, and new punches for the duty mark, lion and leopard head were brought in (*Fig. 102*). After this, the duty punch remained unchanged until 1st May 1890, when duty was totally abolished.

Through the next series of date letter runs, the lion passant and leopard's head shield shapes matched each other, but were changed for each run. It is possible to roughly date items of this period with only one of the three marks readable.

From 1867, any imported silver had to be assayed for sale and was struck with an F in an oval (*Fig. 103*). This changed again in 1904, with new town marks.

Fig. 103 *Foreign import mark 1893*

Fig. 104 *Import marks Chester 1906*

Extra optional marks occurred in 1934/5 and 1935/6 (*Fig. 124*), to celebrate the Jubilee; 1952/3 and 1953/4 the coronation of Queen Elizabeth, and 1977 for her Jubilee (*Fig. 120*).

Fig. 105 *London 1789 "o"*

Fig. 106 *London 1809 "O"*

The dates for *Figs.105 & 106* could be confused at first glance. Due to wear on the marks, are they 1789, 1809 or even 1829, with a date letter of "O" or "o"? As they are teaspoons, the leopard's head is missing. This immediately rules out 1829, as stubs were used on all items from 1821, giving the full set of marks.

Fig. 105 is 1789, with the larger lion, in a shield with a rounded base, and thinner letter. *Fig. 106* is 1809 displaying the smaller version of the lion.

Chester, Exeter, Newcastle and York similarly dispensed with town marks on smaller spoons during George III's reign. These are often confused with London items, unless they are seen side by side.

London punched the date letter between the lion and the duty mark, with the maker's mark usually on the right. Another indicator is that provincial lions were much cruder than those of London, though, in all cases, lion passant guardant.

Fig.107 *Chester1810*

Fig. 108 *Exeter 1810*

Fig. 109 *York 1803*

Fig. 110 *York 1830*

Fig. 111 *Newcastle 1797*

Fig. 112 *Newcastle 1795*

Birmingham

The order in which Birmingham's marks were struck, was very variable for the first few years. The leopard's head was never used. Later the order struck, with the bowl held in the left hand, reading from the right became:

1. The maker or sponsor's mark.
2. The lion passant guardant from 1773 until 1874, when they used the lion passant up to the present date.
3. An anchor in a shield. The shape of the shield has varied over alphabetical runs and is in its fourth pattern now.
4. The date letter.
5. Other marks found on pieces are:
   a) The Duty mark.
   b) Optional marks added to celebrate Jubilees and the Coronation of Queen Elizabeth II.

Birmingham used all twenty-six letters from the start, using a different font for each run. Shields for the anchor and lion passant were also changed.

Fig. 113 *1776 spoon marks, Birmingham*

Fig. 114 *1820 marks*

The date letters from 1891 to 1899 are between the anchor and the lion with flat-sided shield shapes (*Fig. 115*). The next run, 1900–1924, uses lower case letters, and 1925–1949 has upper case ones. Both have shields with convoluted bases (*Fig. 116*). The letters which can be confused in these two runs are o/O, s/S

31

and v/V. The indicator here is the maker's mark, and the fact that far more silver was assayed in the earlier run.

Fig. 115 *1895*

Fig. 116 *1909*

Sheffield

Fig. 117 *Sheffield table spoon 1806*

Fig. 118 *Georgian teaspoon 1809*

Sheffield also excluded the leopard's head. For the first few years, the Office had no strict order of marks. Nowadays they are struck in the following order, from right to left:
1. The maker or sponsor's mark.
2. The date letter (from 1780 until 1853, on small items, the date letter and the crown were in the same punch *Fig. 118*).
3. Lion passant guardant, always.
4. A crown.
5. Other marks found on pieces are:-
    a. The Duty mark.
    b. Optional marks added to celebrate Jubilees and the Coronation of Queen Elizabeth II (*Fig. 120*).

Fig. 119 *Sheff Victorian 1848*

Fig. 120 *Elizabeth II Jubilee 1977*

From 1773 until 1823/4, the letters were used in a random order, but thereafter in alphabetical order. The town mark was always present, either on its own or incorporated with the date letter. The method of ascertaining the date is by checking on the orientation of the crown. In 1975, the crown was replaced by a rose (*Fig. 120*).

In February 1773, the silversmiths of Sheffield and Birmingham petitioned to have assay offices opened in their towns. Their official reason was that sending plate to Chester or London for assay was disastrous as the roads were atrocious, with goods often being broken or stolen en route.

London Goldsmiths were against the creation of these offices, not least that they could steal designs or undercut prices when the plate was sent to London. Initially, they lobbied violently against the Bill, but Matthew Boulton, representing Birmingham, persuaded the Parliamentary committee to purchase twenty-two pieces of plate, made and assayed in London. As twenty-one of them were found to be sub-standard, the London Goldsmiths opposition soon ceased.

Those in charge of the petition to create these two new Assay Offices did much of their planning in the Crown & Anchor Tavern in the Strand. It is believed that they tossed up for the town marks and Sheffield won, taking the crown as their town mark, Birmingham using the anchor.

After 1700 there were four other Assay Offices in England, Chester (closing in 1962), Exeter & Newcastle (closed in 1883), and York (virtually closed in 1856). In 1851, after an official inspection of all the provincial Assay Offices, these four were all found to be producing substandard silver plate. The inspectors stated that the Goldsmiths Halls at Exeter, Newcastle and York were all "ill-conducted ... Incapable of improvement ... and should be immediately suppressed". The commissioners also "recommended that the Hall at Chester should be discontinued".

Chester

For many years, punches used by the Chester Assay Office were struck in a random order, eventually, a standard sequence was adopted. The punches used by Chester were as follows:

1. The maker's, or sponsor's, mark.
2. The Lion passant, always guardant.
3. The City Mark. This initially consisted of a shield with three lions passant on the left half and the town mark of three wheat-sheaves and a sword, only half displayed, on the right (*Fig. 145*). The Royal coat of arms was present because the monarch's eldest son was Earl of Chester as well as Prince of Wales. This punch was used from 1701 to 1778. In 1778, the town mark punch reverted to the present one of three wheat-sheaves with a sword erect between them.
4. The date letter.
5. The crowned leopard's head was struck from 1720 to 1809. This was replaced by an uncrowned leopard's head until 1839 and then ceased.
6. The duty mark from 1784 until 1890 and optional jubilee mark in 1934/5 and 1935/6, plus the coronation mark in 1952/3 and 1953/4.

Fig. 121 Chester Georgian, full 1833   *Fig. 122* Victorian Chester 1841

The Assay Office closed on the 24ᵗʰ August 1962. Before 1900, Chester often did not use the town mark on smaller pieces, giving some confusion with London. Easy identification is by the duty mark. From 1786 – 1834, the shape of the punch conformed to the bust, unlike London. Another difference from London was that the Chester leopard head lost its crown in 1809.

Fig. 123 1923   *Fig. 124* Geo V Jubilee 1935

Exeter

Fig. 125 Exeter marks 1827 (right)   *Fig. 126* Exeter 1856 (left)

Early Exeter marks were punched in a very haphazard order. From 1780 until 1860, they were usually punched left handed (*Figs. 125 & 126*). The following marks were used:-
1. The town mark, a triple towered castle, turreted (signifying Rougemont Castle, Exeter).
2. The lion passant guardant.
3. The duty mark from 1784 until the end in June 1883.
4. The date letter.
5. The maker or sponsor's mark.
6. The crowned leopard's head was only used from 1720 until 1779.
On smaller pieces, the town mark was left off, as well as, occasionally, the date letter. The lion passant guardant for Exeter had no dimple at the bottom of the shield. The other way of identifying a piece like this is from the maker's punch.

Newcastle

The Newcastle marks were:
1. The maker or sponsor's mark.

2. The duty mark from 1784 until the end in 1884.
3. The lion passant, head to the right 1721 and 1723-1727. The lion passant regardant head to the left 1722 and 1728-1809 (*Fig. 127*). Lion passant 1809-1815; regardant 1815-1846; passant 1846 until the closure in May 1884 (*Figs. 129 & 130*).
4. The town mark of three castles. The significance of three castles is not fully understood, but may be the three stages of the castle, Roman, Norman wooden, and, finally, stone.
5. The leopard's head crowned from 1721 until 1884. The uncrowned leopard's head was also used from 1846 to 1884, during which time, both were in use (*Figs. 129 & 130*).
6. The date letter.

In Georgian teaspoons, the town mark was often left off, sometimes the date letter, and also the leopard's head, leaving as few as three marks.

Fig. 127 *Newcastle 1801*   ***Fig. 128*** *Newcastle tea c1793*

Fig. 129 *Newcastle leopard uncrowned*   ***Fig. 130*** *Leopard with crowned head*

York

Fig. 131 *York 1807 Tablespoon*

The York assay office operated until 1716, at which time it was closed due to the lack of plate being made. In 1776, it was re-established, remaining open until 1859.

In 1851, the Assay Master was a retired spoon maker, named John Burrill. He ran a pub, having the Assay Office in a back room. He had no understanding of how to do the job, but was retained in post by the two Wardens, who were also the producers of all the plate in York. He was unable to test the purity of the silver and always took their word for it.

Fig. 132 *York 1818 teaspoon*   **Fig. 133** *York Victorian*

During the Nineteenth Century, the marks were:

1. The sponsor's mark.
2. The lion passant.
3. The duty mark from 1784 until the close in 1859.
4. The crowned leopard's head (on larger pieces).
5. The date letter.
6. The town mark of a cross with five lions (when used, it is very unusual to get the town mark on flatware [*Fig. 146*].)

Spoons are the most commonly found examples of York silver from the Nineteenth Century and these are often confused with London examples.

The easily noted differences are that the York makers' marks, associated with the most prolific makers, were punched to be read with the bowl in the hand and the stem vertical (*Fig. 132*). London pieces were marked so that they would be read with the bowl in the left hand, stem horizontal (*Fig. 106*). When applied, York used the crowned leopard head until closure, also their punches were of much poorer quality.

For further information on the other towns in England operating prior to 1700, see "*Jackson's Silver & Gold Marks of England, Scotland & Ireland*".

Edinburgh

Edinburgh is the fourth assay office still operating, with the following marks:

1. The maker or sponsor's mark.
2. The town mark of a triple towered castle, taken from the City coat of arms. The castle mark varied been 1799 to 1826. It has been surmised that there were two assayers working, one with a punch with pointed towers, the other with flat topped towers. This latter mark is sometimes confused with the Exeter castle. If there is a lion passant present in the punches, it will not be Scottish silver.
3. A thistle, denoting the fact that the item had been assayed and the metal was of the required standard, used in Scotland instead of the lion passant.
4. The date letter.
5. The monarch's head duty mark, used from 1784 until 1890. This was also used as an optional jubilee mark in 1934/5 and 1935/6, plus the coronation mark in 1952/3 and 1953/4.

Fig. 134 Edinburgh pointed castle

Fig. 135 Edinburgh flat castle

Some pieces are struck with two sets of makers' marks. The second mark denoted the seller of the item, usually to the right of the town marks (*Fig. 135*).

Other variations of marks on Edinburgh pieces, including those sent in for assay from provincial makers, were:- maker's mark, date letter, thistle and duty punch; the maker's mark, thistle and duty punch; maker's mark, castle, duty mark (*Figs. 136-138*). *Fig. 138* shows an item from the Zeigler factory, where flatware was often made for selling on in the provincial towns.

It is not uncommon for Scottish silver teaspoons to have a number, between 1 and 12, engraved on the handle, close to the inscription. This ensured that it was easy for a host to identify the guest who had quietly pocketed a piece of silver.

Fig. 136 Castle no thistle

Fig. 137 Thistle no castle or date

Fig. 138 No castle

Fig. 139 Glasgow pre-1800 mark

Glasgow

Glasgow also marked their own gold and silver, using between one and four marks until 1819, when the town became an official Assay Office.

The early marks used were the maker's mark, often twice on larger pieces, sometimes a letter, and the town mark. The town mark was made up of items representing events in the life of St Kentigern also known as St Mungo (*Fig. 139*).

Fig. 140 Glasgow 1819

Fig. 141 Glasgow 1960

These items consisted of a tree, usually represented as an oak, but originally a hazel branch, across the trunk is a salmon. A bell, usually hangs from the right of the tree, sometimes the left, representing one given to St Mungo by the pope. There is a robin perched on the top of the tree. Some smiths also used a G, either hanging from the tree or in the salmon's mouth. Up to 1818, all the punches used to belong to the smith, and depended on their whim. Officially, from 1784 until 1819, all silver was supposed to be assayed in Edinburgh. In 1819 the punches were regularised to the following:

1. The maker's mark.
2. The duty mark from 1819 until 1890.
3. The town mark.
4. The lion rampant denoting that the metal was of the required standard.
5. The date letter.
The Glasgow assay office closed in 1964.

Many of the major towns in Scotland had their own silversmiths, very few of whom paid duty on their silver or gold. Some had their own town marks, a selection of which is shown on pages 39 & 40.

Dublin

 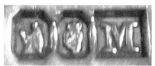

Fig. 142 *Georgian Dublin Marks 1814*   **Fig. 143** *Dublin 1954*

Fig. 144 *Typical marks for Cork, in this case, John Toleken c1810.*

Ireland was part of the United Kingdom until 1916, and Dublin was the assay office for the whole of Ireland, though Cork and Limerick produced a quantity of plate.

The Dublin marks were as follows:
1. Maker's mark.
2. Duty mark from 1807 until 1890.
3. Hibernia.
4. Crowned harp.
5. Date letter
Special commemorative marks were used in 1966, 1973, 1987 and 1988.

General Information

Among items useful to be carried when buying, is a pocket sized book on silver hall marks. (There are two or three very good ones on the market, check to see which suits you.) Another is a jeweller's loupe or eyeglass, or a magnifying glass. One of at least 10x magnification for checking marks and condition is ideal.

There are several sites on line for discovering the origination of silver from its marks. Examples are: http://www.925-1000.com/ http://www.silvercollection.it/

For Scottish marks use http://incorporationofgoldsmiths.co.uk

Places to visit

The Goldsmiths Hall & Assay Office, London http://www.thegoldsmiths.co.uk/ Goldsmiths Hall open days 6 times per year. For this, the Fakes & Forgeries Seminars and Assay Office tours contact Alison Byne Tel 0207606 8971 x3013; email alison.byne@assayofficelondon.co.uk

The Assay Office, New Hall Street, Birmingham http://www.theassayoffice.co.uk/ Tours every Tuesday & Thursday, parties of 10 to 25. Contact Kelly Fisher Tel 44 (0)121 262 1024; email kelly.fisher@theassayoffice.co.uk

The Assay Office, Beulah Road, Hillsborough, Sheffield. http://www.assayoffice.co.uk/

Tours of the Assay Office, contact Emma Paragreen Tel 44 (0) 114 2312121; email ParagreenE@assayoffice.co.uk

The Silver Vaults, Chancery Lane, London http://www.thesilvervaults.com/ Portobello Road, London (Saturday morning). http://www.portobellomarket.org/

Other Town Marks, not previously illustrated

Fig. 145 Chester before 1779

Fig. 146 York

Fig. 147 Aberdeen

Fig. 148 Banff

Fig. 149 *Dumfries*

Fig. 150 *Dundee*

Fig. 151 *Elgin*

Fig. 152 *Greenock*

Fig. 153 *Inverness*

Fig. 154 *Montrose*

Fig. 155 *Perth*

Fig. 156 *Tain*

Bibliography

Collecting Irish Silver	Douglas Bennett
The Finial	Ed: Daniel Bexfield
History of Old Sheffield Plate	Frederick Bradbury
London Gold & Silversmiths 1838–1914	John Culme
Nineteenth Century Silver	John Culme
Exeter & West Country Silver	Exeter Museum
Fairbairn's Book of Crests	Fairbairn
Hallmark, History of the London Assay Office	J S Forbes
Old Silver Spoons of England	Norman Gask
Directory of Newcastle Goldsmiths	M A V Gill
Victorian Electroplaters 1841–1900	Andrea De Giovanni
The Assay Office & Silversmiths of York	Martin Gubbins
The Goldsmiths of Aberdeen	I E James
The Silversmiths of Birmingham	Kenneth Crisp Jones
English Engraved Silver	Charles Oman
Silver Flatware	Ian Pickford
Early English Silver Spoons	Ian Pickford
Jackson's Silver & Gold Marks	Ed. by Ian Pickford
Chester Gold & Silver Marks	Ridgeway & Priestley
English Silver Spoons	Michael Snodin
International Silver Marks	Tardy
Directory of Scottish Provincial Silversmiths	Richard W Turner